PIANO • VOCAL

Kids' Stage & Screen SONGS

Compiled by
LOUISE LERCH

Contents

CHILDREN SINGERS, PREPARED BY LOUISE LERCH:

DEBORAH BILLINGSLY: CANDLE ON THE WATER, FEED THE BIRDS, IN MY OWN LITTLE CORNER

KATHARINE CHAMBERS: DITES-MOI, MAYBE

AMBER EDMUNDS: LET ME ENTERTAIN YOU, A SPOONFUL OF SUGAR

CURRY WHITMIRE: WHO WILL BUY?, I WON'T GROW UP, ZIP-A-DEE-DOO-DAH

LOUISE LERCH, PIANIST

ISBN 0-634-03067-1

HAL•LEONARD®
CORPORATION
7777 W. BLUEMOUND RD. P.O. BOX 13819 MILWAUKEE, WI 53213

Visit Hal Leonard Online at
www.halleonard.com

DITES-MOI
(TELL ME WHY)
from SOUTH PACIFIC

Lyrics by OSCAR HAMMERSTEIN II
Music by RICHARD RODGERS

FEED THE BIRDS

from Walt Disney's MARY POPPINS

Words and Music by RICHARD M. SHERMAN
and ROBERT B. SHERMAN

Slowly, with feeling

VERSE

Ear-ly each day to the steps of Saint Paul's The lit-tle old bird wom-an comes._____ In her own spe-cial way to the peo-ple she calls, "Come, buy my bags full of crumbs;_____

Come feed the lit-tle birds, show them you care And you'll be

glad if you do;_____ Their young ones are hun-gry, their

nests are so bare; All it takes is tup-pence from you._____

CHORUS

Feed ____ the birds, tup-pence ____ a bag, Tup-pence,____

I WON'T GROW UP

from PETER PAN

Lyric by CAROLYN LEIGH
Music by MARK CHARLAP

IN MY OWN LITTLE CORNER

from CINDERELLA

Lyrics by OSCAR HAMMERSTEIN II
Music by RICHARD RODGERS

CANDLE ON THE WATER

from Walt Disney's PETE'S DRAGON

Words and Music by AL KASHA
and JOEL HIRSCHHORN

LET ME ENTERTAIN YOU

from GYPSY

Words by STEPHEN SONDHEIM
Music by JULE STYNE

MAYBE
from the Musical Production ANNIE

Lyric by MARTIN CHARNIN
Music by CHARLES STROUSE

WHO WILL BUY?
from the Columbia Pictures - Romulus Film OLIVER!

Words and Music by
LIONEL BART

ZIP-A-DEE-DOO-DAH
from Walt Disney's SONG OF THE SOUTH

Words by RAY GILBERT
Music by ALLIE WRUBEL

A SPOONFUL OF SUGAR

from Walt Disney's MARY POPPINS

Words and Music by
RICHARD M. SHERMAN
and ROBERT B. SHERMAN